Amendment to Trust

Legally Binding

Trusts Legal Forms Book

Amendment to Trust

Review List

This review list is provided to inform you about this document in question and assist you in its preparation. Sign amendments in the same manner as you did the original trust. All parties should sign and the signatures notarized for your protection. Be sure to initial each page.

1. Make multiple copies. Keep copies of amendments with all originals.

Amendment to Trust

1, _____, ("Grantor") of _____, hereby amend _____

("Trust") as follows: _____.

Except as expressly modified by this Amendment I approve, ratify and affirm the Trust.

Date:

_____

Grantor

_____

Trustee

STATE OF _____

COUNTY OF _____

This instrument was acknowledged before me on this __ day of _____, 20__ by Grantor, _____ and Trustee, _____.

_____

Notary Public

My Commission Expires on:

Amendment to Trust

1, _____, ("Grantor") of _____, hereby amend _____

("Trust") as follows: _____.

Except as expressly modified by this Amendment I approve, ratify and affirm the Trust.

Date:

_____
Grantor

_____
Trustee

STATE OF _____

COUNTY OF _____

This instrument was acknowledged before me on this __ day of _____, 20__ by Grantor,

_____ and Trustee, _____.

_____
Notary Public

My Commission Expires on:

Amendment to Trust

1, _____, ("Grantor") of _____, hereby amend _____ ("Trust") as follows: _____.

Except as expressly modified by this Amendment I approve, ratify and affirm the Trust.

Date:

_____

Grantor

_____

Trustee

STATE OF _____

COUNTY OF _____

This instrument was acknowledged before me on this __ day of _____, 20__ by Grantor, _____ and Trustee, _____.

_____

Notary Public

My Commission Expires on:

Amendment to Trust

1, _____, ("Grantor") of _____, hereby amend _____

("Trust") as follows: _____.

Except as expressly modified by this Amendment I approve, ratify and affirm the Trust.

Date:

_____

Grantor

_____

Trustee

STATE OF _____

COUNTY OF _____

This instrument was acknowledged before me on this __ day of _____, 20__ by Grantor, _____ and Trustee, _____.

_____

Notary Public

My Commission Expires on:

Amendment to Trust

1, _____, ("Grantor") of _____, hereby amend _____ ("Trust") as follows: _____.

Except as expressly modified by this Amendment I approve, ratify and affirm the Trust.

Date:

_____
Grantor

_____
Trustee

STATE OF _____

COUNTY OF _____

This instrument was acknowledged before me on this __ day of _____, 20__ by Grantor, _____ and Trustee, _____.

_____
Notary Public

My Commission Expires on:

Amendment to Trust

1, _____, ("Grantor") of _____, hereby amend _____

("Trust") as follows: _____.

Except as expressly modified by this Amendment I approve, ratify and affirm the Trust.

Date:

_____
Grantor

_____
Trustee

STATE OF _____

COUNTY OF _____

This instrument was acknowledged before me on this __ day of _____, 20__ by Grantor, _____ and Trustee, _____.

_____
Notary Public

My Commission Expires on:

Amendment to Trust

1, _____, ("Grantor") of _____, hereby amend _____

("Trust") as follows: _____.

Except as expressly modified by this Amendment I approve, ratify and affirm the Trust.

Date:

_____

Grantor

_____

Trustee

STATE OF _____

COUNTY OF _____

This instrument was acknowledged before me on this __ day of _____, 20__ by Grantor, _____ and Trustee, _____.

_____

Notary Public

My Commission Expires on:

Amendment to Trust

1, _____, ("Grantor") of _____, hereby amend _____

("Trust") as follows: _____.

Except as expressly modified by this Amendment I approve, ratify and affirm the Trust.

Date:

_____
Grantor

_____
Trustee

STATE OF _____

COUNTY OF _____

This instrument was acknowledged before me on this __ day of _____, 20__ by Grantor,

_____ and Trustee, _____.

_____
Notary Public

My Commission Expires on:

Amendment to Trust

1, _____, ("Grantor") of _____, hereby amend _____

("Trust") as follows: _____.

Except as expressly modified by this Amendment I approve, ratify and affirm the Trust.

Date:

_____

Grantor

_____

Trustee

STATE OF _____

COUNTY OF _____

This instrument was acknowledged before me on this __ day of _____, 20__ by Grantor, _____ and Trustee, _____.

_____

Notary Public

My Commission Expires on:

Amendment to Trust

1, _____, ("Grantor") of _____, hereby amend _____

("Trust") as follows: _____.

Except as expressly modified by this Amendment I approve, ratify and affirm the Trust.

Date:

_____

Grantor

_____

Trustee

STATE OF _____

COUNTY OF _____

This instrument was acknowledged before me on this __ day of _____, 20__ by Grantor, _____ and Trustee, _____.

_____

Notary Public

My Commission Expires on:

Amendment to Trust

1, _____, ("Grantor") of _____, hereby amend _____

("Trust") as follows: _____.

Except as expressly modified by this Amendment I approve, ratify and affirm the Trust.

Date:

_____

Grantor

_____

Trustee

STATE OF _____

COUNTY OF _____

This instrument was acknowledged before me on this __ day of _____, 20__ by Grantor,

_____ and Trustee, _____.

_____

Notary Public

My Commission Expires on:

Amendment to Trust

1, _____, ("Grantor") of _____, hereby amend _____

("Trust") as follows: _____.

Except as expressly modified by this Amendment I approve, ratify and affirm the Trust.

Date:

_____

Grantor

_____

Trustee

STATE OF _____

COUNTY OF _____

This instrument was acknowledged before me on this __ day of _____, 20__ by Grantor,

_____ and Trustee, _____.

_____

Notary Public

My Commission Expires on:

Amendment to Trust

1, _____, ("Grantor") of _____, hereby amend _____

("Trust") as follows: _____.

Except as expressly modified by this Amendment I approve, ratify and affirm the Trust.

Date:

_____

Grantor

_____

Trustee

STATE OF _____

COUNTY OF _____

This instrument was acknowledged before me on this __ day of _____, 20__ by Grantor,

_____ and Trustee, _____.

_____

Notary Public

My Commission Expires on:

Amendment to Trust

1, _____, ("Grantor") of _____, hereby amend _____

("Trust") as follows: _____.

Except as expressly modified by this Amendment I approve, ratify and affirm the Trust.

Date:

_____

Grantor

_____

Trustee

STATE OF _____

COUNTY OF _____

This instrument was acknowledged before me on this __ day of _____, 20__ by Grantor, _____ and Trustee, _____.

_____

Notary Public

My Commission Expires on:

Amendment to Trust

1, _____, ("Grantor") of _____, hereby amend _____ ("Trust") as follows: _____.

Except as expressly modified by this Amendment I approve, ratify and affirm the Trust.

Date:

_____

Grantor

_____

Trustee

STATE OF _____

COUNTY OF _____

This instrument was acknowledged before me on this __ day of _____, 20__ by Grantor, _____ and Trustee, _____.

_____

Notary Public

My Commission Expires on:

Amendment to Trust

1, _____, ("Grantor") of _____, hereby amend _____ ("Trust") as follows: _____.

Except as expressly modified by this Amendment I approve, ratify and affirm the Trust.

Date:

_____

Grantor

_____

Trustee

STATE OF _____

COUNTY OF _____

This instrument was acknowledged before me on this __ day of _____, 20__ by Grantor, _____ and Trustee, _____.

_____

Notary Public

My Commission Expires on:

Amendment to Trust

1, _____, ("Grantor") of _____, hereby amend _____ ("Trust") as follows: _____.

Except as expressly modified by this Amendment I approve, ratify and affirm the Trust.

Date:

_____
Grantor

_____
Trustee

STATE OF _____

COUNTY OF _____

This instrument was acknowledged before me on this __ day of _____, 20__ by Grantor, _____ and Trustee, _____.

_____
Notary Public

My Commission Expires on:

Amendment to Trust

1, _____, ("Grantor") of _____, hereby amend _____ ("Trust") as follows: _____.

Except as expressly modified by this Amendment I approve, ratify and affirm the Trust.

Date:

_____

Grantor

_____

Trustee

STATE OF _____

COUNTY OF _____

This instrument was acknowledged before me on this __ day of _____, 20__ by Grantor, _____ and Trustee, _____.

_____

Notary Public

My Commission Expires on:

Amendment to Trust

1, _____, ("Grantor") of _____, hereby amend _____

("Trust") as follows: _____.

Except as expressly modified by this Amendment I approve, ratify and affirm the Trust.

Date:

_____

Grantor

_____

Trustee

STATE OF _____

COUNTY OF _____

This instrument was acknowledged before me on this __ day of _____, 20__ by Grantor, _____ and Trustee, _____.

_____

Notary Public

My Commission Expires on:

Amendment to Trust

1, _____, ("Grantor") of _____, hereby amend _____

("Trust") as follows: _____.

Except as expressly modified by this Amendment I approve, ratify and affirm the Trust.

Date:

_____

Grantor

_____

Trustee

STATE OF _____

COUNTY OF _____

This instrument was acknowledged before me on this __ day of _____, 20__ by Grantor, _____ and Trustee, _____.

_____

Notary Public

My Commission Expires on:

Amendment to Trust

1, _____, ("Grantor") of _____, hereby amend _____ ("Trust") as follows: _____.

Except as expressly modified by this Amendment I approve, ratify and affirm the Trust.

Date:

_____

Grantor

_____

Trustee

STATE OF _____

COUNTY OF _____

This instrument was acknowledged before me on this __ day of _____, 20__ by Grantor, _____ and Trustee, _____.

_____

Notary Public

My Commission Expires on:

Amendment to Trust

1, _____, ("Grantor") of _____, hereby amend _____ ("Trust") as follows: _____.

Except as expressly modified by this Amendment I approve, ratify and affirm the Trust.

Date:

_____
Grantor

_____
Trustee

STATE OF _____

COUNTY OF _____

This instrument was acknowledged before me on this __ day of _____, 20__ by Grantor, _____ and Trustee, _____.

_____
Notary Public

My Commission Expires on:

Amendment to Trust

1, _____, ("Grantor") of _____, hereby amend _____ ("Trust") as follows: _____.

Except as expressly modified by this Amendment I approve, ratify and affirm the Trust.

Date:

_____
Grantor

_____
Trustee

STATE OF _____

COUNTY OF _____

This instrument was acknowledged before me on this __ day of _____, 20__ by Grantor, _____ and Trustee, _____.

_____
Notary Public

My Commission Expires on:

Amendment to Trust

1, _____, ("Grantor") of _____, hereby amend _____

("Trust") as follows: _____.

Except as expressly modified by this Amendment I approve, ratify and affirm the Trust.

Date:

_____

Grantor

_____

Trustee

STATE OF _____

COUNTY OF _____

This instrument was acknowledged before me on this __ day of _____, 20__ by Grantor,

_____ and Trustee, _____.

_____

Notary Public

My Commission Expires on:

Amendment to Trust

1, _____, ("Grantor") of _____, hereby amend _____ ("Trust") as follows: _____.

Except as expressly modified by this Amendment I approve, ratify and affirm the Trust.

Date:

_____

Grantor

_____

Trustee

STATE OF _____

COUNTY OF _____

This instrument was acknowledged before me on this __ day of _____, 20__ by Grantor, _____ and Trustee, _____.

_____

Notary Public

My Commission Expires on:

Amendment to Trust

1, _____, ("Grantor") of _____, hereby amend _____

("Trust") as follows: _____.

Except as expressly modified by this Amendment I approve, ratify and affirm the Trust.

Date:

_____

Grantor

_____

Trustee

STATE OF _____

COUNTY OF _____

This instrument was acknowledged before me on this __ day of _____, 20__ by Grantor,

_____ and Trustee, _____.

_____

Notary Public

My Commission Expires on:

Amendment to Trust

1, _____, ("Grantor") of _____, hereby amend _____

("Trust") as follows: _____.

Except as expressly modified by this Amendment I approve, ratify and affirm the Trust.

Date:

_____

Grantor

_____

Trustee

STATE OF _____

COUNTY OF _____

This instrument was acknowledged before me on this __ day of _____, 20__ by Grantor,

_____ and Trustee, _____.

_____

Notary Public

My Commission Expires on:

Amendment to Trust

1, _____, ("Grantor") of _____, hereby amend _____

("Trust") as follows: _____.

Except as expressly modified by this Amendment I approve, ratify and affirm the Trust.

Date:

_____

Grantor

_____

Trustee

STATE OF _____

COUNTY OF _____

This instrument was acknowledged before me on this ___ day of _____, 20___ by Grantor,

_____ and Trustee, _____.

_____

Notary Public

My Commission Expires on:

Amendment to Trust

1, _____, ("Grantor") of _____, hereby amend _____

("Trust") as follows: _____.

Except as expressly modified by this Amendment I approve, ratify and affirm the Trust.

Date:

_____

Grantor

_____

Trustee

STATE OF _____

COUNTY OF _____

This instrument was acknowledged before me on this __ day of _____, 20__ by Grantor, _____ and Trustee, _____.

_____

Notary Public

My Commission Expires on:

Amendment to Trust

1, _____, ("Grantor") of _____, hereby amend _____ ("Trust") as follows: _____.

Except as expressly modified by this Amendment I approve, ratify and affirm the Trust.

Date:

_____
Grantor

_____
Trustee

STATE OF _____

COUNTY OF _____

This instrument was acknowledged before me on this __ day of _____, 20__ by Grantor, _____ and Trustee, _____.

_____
Notary Public

My Commission Expires on:

Amendment to Trust

1, _____, ("Grantor") of _____, hereby amend _____
("Trust") as follows: _____.

Except as expressly modified by this Amendment I approve, ratify and affirm the Trust.

Date:

_____
Grantor

_____
Trustee

STATE OF _____
COUNTY OF _____

This instrument was acknowledged before me on this __ day of _____, 20__ by Grantor, _____ and Trustee, _____.

_____
Notary Public

My Commission Expires on:

Amendment to Trust

1, _____, ("Grantor") of _____, hereby amend _____

("Trust") as follows: _____.

Except as expressly modified by this Amendment I approve, ratify and affirm the Trust.

Date:

_____

Grantor

_____

Trustee

STATE OF _____

COUNTY OF _____

This instrument was acknowledged before me on this __ day of _____, 20__ by Grantor, _____ and Trustee, _____.

_____

Notary Public

My Commission Expires on:

Amendment to Trust

1, _____, ("Grantor") of _____, hereby amend _____

("Trust") as follows: _____.

Except as expressly modified by this Amendment I approve, ratify and affirm the Trust.

Date:

_____

Grantor

_____

Trustee

STATE OF _____

COUNTY OF _____

This instrument was acknowledged before me on this __ day of _____, 20__ by Grantor,

_____ and Trustee, _____.

_____

Notary Public

My Commission Expires on:

Amendment to Trust

1, _____, ("Grantor") of _____, hereby amend _____ ("Trust") as follows: _____.

Except as expressly modified by this Amendment I approve, ratify and affirm the Trust.

Date:

_____

Grantor

_____

Trustee

STATE OF _____

COUNTY OF _____

This instrument was acknowledged before me on this __ day of _____, 20__ by Grantor, _____ and Trustee, _____.

_____

Notary Public

My Commission Expires on:

Amendment to Trust

1, _____, ("Grantor") of _____, hereby amend _____

("Trust") as follows: _____.

Except as expressly modified by this Amendment I approve, ratify and affirm the Trust.

Date:

_____

Grantor

_____

Trustee

STATE OF _____

COUNTY OF _____

This instrument was acknowledged before me on this __ day of _____, 20__ by Grantor, _____ and Trustee, _____.

_____

Notary Public

My Commission Expires on:

Amendment to Trust

1, _____, ("Grantor") of _____, hereby amend _____

("Trust") as follows: _____.

Except as expressly modified by this Amendment I approve, ratify and affirm the Trust.

Date:

_____

Grantor

_____

Trustee

STATE OF _____

COUNTY OF _____

This instrument was acknowledged before me on this __ day of _____, 20__ by Grantor, _____ and Trustee, _____.

_____

Notary Public

My Commission Expires on:

Amendment to Trust

1, _____, ("Grantor") of _____, hereby amend _____

("Trust") as follows: _____.

Except as expressly modified by this Amendment I approve, ratify and affirm the Trust.

Date:

_____

Grantor

_____

Trustee

STATE OF _____

COUNTY OF _____

This instrument was acknowledged before me on this __ day of _____, 20__ by Grantor,

_____ and Trustee, _____.

_____

Notary Public

My Commission Expires on:

Amendment to Trust

1, _____, ("Grantor") of _____, hereby amend _____

("Trust") as follows: _____.

Except as expressly modified by this Amendment I approve, ratify and affirm the Trust.

Date:

_____

Grantor

_____

Trustee

STATE OF _____

COUNTY OF _____

This instrument was acknowledged before me on this __ day of _____, 20__ by Grantor, _____ and Trustee, _____.

_____

Notary Public

My Commission Expires on:

Amendment to Trust

1, _____, ("Grantor") of _____, hereby amend _____

("Trust") as follows: _____.

Except as expressly modified by this Amendment I approve, ratify and affirm the Trust.

Date:

_____

Grantor

_____

Trustee

STATE OF _____

COUNTY OF _____

This instrument was acknowledged before me on this __ day of _____, 20__ by Grantor,

_____ and Trustee, _____.

_____

Notary Public

My Commission Expires on:

Amendment to Trust

1, _____, ("Grantor") of _____, hereby amend _____

("Trust") as follows: _____.

Except as expressly modified by this Amendment I approve, ratify and affirm the Trust.

Date:

_____

Grantor

_____

Trustee

STATE OF _____

COUNTY OF _____

This instrument was acknowledged before me on this __ day of _____, 20__ by Grantor, _____ and Trustee, _____.

_____

Notary Public

My Commission Expires on:

Amendment to Trust

1, _____, ("Grantor") of _____, hereby amend _____ ("Trust") as follows: _____.

Except as expressly modified by this Amendment I approve, ratify and affirm the Trust.

Date:

_____
Grantor

_____
Trustee

STATE OF _____

COUNTY OF _____

This instrument was acknowledged before me on this __ day of _____, 20__ by Grantor, _____ and Trustee, _____.

_____
Notary Public

My Commission Expires on:

Amendment to Trust

1, _____, ("Grantor") of _____, hereby amend _____

("Trust") as follows: _____.

Except as expressly modified by this Amendment I approve, ratify and affirm the Trust.

Date:

_____

Grantor

_____

Trustee

STATE OF _____

COUNTY OF _____

This instrument was acknowledged before me on this __ day of _____, 20__ by Grantor, _____ and Trustee, _____.

_____

Notary Public

My Commission Expires on:

Amendment to Trust

1, _____, ("Grantor") of _____, hereby amend _____

("Trust") as follows: _____.

Except as expressly modified by this Amendment I approve, ratify and affirm the Trust.

Date:

_____

Grantor

_____

Trustee

STATE OF _____

COUNTY OF _____

This instrument was acknowledged before me on this __ day of _____, 20__ by Grantor,

_____ and Trustee, _____.

_____

Notary Public

My Commission Expires on:

Amendment to Trust

1, _____, ("Grantor") of _____, hereby amend _____ ("Trust") as follows: _____.

Except as expressly modified by this Amendment I approve, ratify and affirm the Trust.

Date:

_____

Grantor

_____

Trustee

STATE OF _____

COUNTY OF _____

This instrument was acknowledged before me on this __ day of _____, 20__ by Grantor, _____ and Trustee, _____.

_____

Notary Public

My Commission Expires on:

Amendment to Trust

1, _____, ("Grantor") of _____, hereby amend _____ ("Trust") as follows: _____.

Except as expressly modified by this Amendment I approve, ratify and affirm the Trust.

Date:

_____
Grantor

_____
Trustee

STATE OF _____

COUNTY OF _____

This instrument was acknowledged before me on this __ day of _____, 20__ by Grantor, _____ and Trustee, _____.

_____
Notary Public

My Commission Expires on:

Amendment to Trust

1, _____, ("Grantor") of _____, hereby amend _____

("Trust") as follows: _____.

Except as expressly modified by this Amendment I approve, ratify and affirm the Trust.

Date:

_____
Grantor

_____
Trustee

STATE OF _____

COUNTY OF _____

This instrument was acknowledged before me on this __ day of _____, 20__ by Grantor, _____ and Trustee, _____.

_____
Notary Public

My Commission Expires on:

Amendment to Trust

1, _____, ("Grantor") of _____, hereby amend _____

("Trust") as follows: _____.

Except as expressly modified by this Amendment I approve, ratify and affirm the Trust.

Date:

_____

Grantor

_____

Trustee

STATE OF _____

COUNTY OF _____

This instrument was acknowledged before me on this __ day of _____, 20__ by Grantor, _____ and Trustee, _____.

_____

Notary Public

My Commission Expires on:

Amendment to Trust

1, _____, ("Grantor") of _____, hereby amend _____ ("Trust") as follows: _____.

Except as expressly modified by this Amendment I approve, ratify and affirm the Trust.

Date:

_____

Grantor

_____

Trustee

STATE OF _____

COUNTY OF _____

This instrument was acknowledged before me on this __ day of _____, 20__ by Grantor, _____ and Trustee, _____.

_____

Notary Public

My Commission Expires on:

Amendment to Trust

1, _____, ("Grantor") of _____, hereby amend _____
("Trust") as follows: _____.

Except as expressly modified by this Amendment I approve, ratify and affirm the Trust.

Date:

_____
Grantor

_____
Trustee

STATE OF _____

COUNTY OF _____

This instrument was acknowledged before me on this __ day of _____, 20__ by Grantor, _____ and Trustee, _____.

_____
Notary Public

My Commission Expires on:

Amendment to Trust

1, _____, ("Grantor") of _____, hereby amend _____

("Trust") as follows: _____.

Except as expressly modified by this Amendment I approve, ratify and affirm the Trust.

Date:

_____

Grantor

_____

Trustee

STATE OF _____

COUNTY OF _____

This instrument was acknowledged before me on this __ day of _____, 20__ by Grantor,

_____ and Trustee, _____.

_____

Notary Public

My Commission Expires on:

Amendment to Trust

1, _____, ("Grantor") of _____, hereby amend _____

("Trust") as follows: _____.

Except as expressly modified by this Amendment I approve, ratify and affirm the Trust.

Date:

_____

Grantor

_____

Trustee

STATE OF _____

COUNTY OF _____

This instrument was acknowledged before me on this __ day of _____, 20__ by Grantor, _____ and Trustee, _____.

_____

Notary Public

My Commission Expires on:

Amendment to Trust

1, _____, ("Grantor") of _____, hereby amend _____ ("Trust") as follows: _____.

Except as expressly modified by this Amendment I approve, ratify and affirm the Trust.

Date:

_____

Grantor

_____

Trustee

STATE OF _____

COUNTY OF _____

This instrument was acknowledged before me on this __ day of _____, 20__ by Grantor, _____ and Trustee, _____.

_____

Notary Public

My Commission Expires on:

Amendment to Trust

1, _____, ("Grantor") of _____, hereby amend _____ ("Trust") as follows: _____.

Except as expressly modified by this Amendment I approve, ratify and affirm the Trust.

Date:

_____
Grantor

_____
Trustee

STATE OF _____

COUNTY OF _____

This instrument was acknowledged before me on this __ day of _____, 20__ by Grantor, _____ and Trustee, _____.

_____
Notary Public

My Commission Expires on:

Amendment to Trust

1, _____, ("Grantor") of _____, hereby amend _____ ("Trust") as follows: _____.

Except as expressly modified by this Amendment I approve, ratify and affirm the Trust.

Date:

_____

Grantor

_____

Trustee

STATE OF _____

COUNTY OF _____

This instrument was acknowledged before me on this __ day of _____, 20__ by Grantor, _____ and Trustee, _____.

_____

Notary Public

My Commission Expires on:

Amendment to Trust

1, _____, ("Grantor") of _____, hereby amend _____

("Trust") as follows: _____.

Except as expressly modified by this Amendment I approve, ratify and affirm the Trust.

Date:

_____

Grantor

_____

Trustee

STATE OF _____

COUNTY OF _____

This instrument was acknowledged before me on this __ day of _____, 20__ by Grantor, _____ and Trustee, _____.

_____

Notary Public

My Commission Expires on:

Amendment to Trust

1, _____, ("Grantor") of _____, hereby amend _____ ("Trust") as follows: _____.

Except as expressly modified by this Amendment I approve, ratify and affirm the Trust.

Date:

_____

Grantor

_____

Trustee

STATE OF _____

COUNTY OF _____

This instrument was acknowledged before me on this __ day of _____, 20__ by Grantor, _____ and Trustee, _____.

_____

Notary Public

My Commission Expires on:

Amendment to Trust

1, _____, ("Grantor") of _____, hereby amend _____

("Trust") as follows: _____.

Except as expressly modified by this Amendment I approve, ratify and affirm the Trust.

Date:

_____

Grantor

_____

Trustee

STATE OF _____

COUNTY OF _____

This instrument was acknowledged before me on this __ day of _____, 20__ by Grantor, _____ and Trustee, _____.

_____

Notary Public

My Commission Expires on:

Amendment to Trust

1, _____, ("Grantor") of _____, hereby amend _____

("Trust") as follows: _____.

Except as expressly modified by this Amendment I approve, ratify and affirm the Trust.

Date:

_____

Grantor

_____

Trustee

STATE OF _____

COUNTY OF _____

This instrument was acknowledged before me on this __ day of _____, 20__ by Grantor, _____ and Trustee, _____.

_____

Notary Public

My Commission Expires on:

Amendment to Trust

1, _____, ("Grantor") of _____, hereby amend _____

("Trust") as follows: _____.

Except as expressly modified by this Amendment I approve, ratify and affirm the Trust.

Date:

_____

Grantor

_____

Trustee

STATE OF _____

COUNTY OF _____

This instrument was acknowledged before me on this __ day of _____, 20__ by Grantor, _____ and Trustee, _____.

_____

Notary Public

My Commission Expires on:

Amendment to Trust

1, _____, ("Grantor") of _____, hereby amend _____ ("Trust") as follows: _____.

Except as expressly modified by this Amendment I approve, ratify and affirm the Trust.

Date:

_____

Grantor

_____

Trustee

STATE OF _____

COUNTY OF _____

This instrument was acknowledged before me on this __ day of _____, 20__ by Grantor, _____ and Trustee, _____.

_____

Notary Public

My Commission Expires on:

Amendment to Trust

1, _____, ("Grantor") of _____, hereby amend _____
("Trust") as follows: _____.

Except as expressly modified by this Amendment I approve, ratify and affirm the Trust.

Date:

_____
Grantor

_____
Trustee

STATE OF _____

COUNTY OF _____

This instrument was acknowledged before me on this __ day of _____, 20__ by Grantor, _____ and Trustee, _____.

_____
Notary Public

My Commission Expires on:

Amendment to Trust

1, _____, ("Grantor") of _____, hereby amend _____ ("Trust") as follows: _____.

Except as expressly modified by this Amendment I approve, ratify and affirm the Trust.

Date:

_____

Grantor

_____

Trustee

STATE OF _____

COUNTY OF _____

This instrument was acknowledged before me on this __ day of _____, 20__ by Grantor, _____ and Trustee, _____.

_____

Notary Public

My Commission Expires on:

Amendment to Trust

1, _____, ("Grantor") of _____, hereby amend _____

("Trust") as follows: _____.

Except as expressly modified by this Amendment I approve, ratify and affirm the Trust.

Date:

_____
Grantor

_____
Trustee

STATE OF _____

COUNTY OF _____

This instrument was acknowledged before me on this __ day of _____, 20__ by Grantor, _____ and Trustee, _____.

_____
Notary Public

My Commission Expires on:

Amendment to Trust

1, _____, ("Grantor") of _____, hereby amend _____ ("Trust") as follows: _____.

Except as expressly modified by this Amendment I approve, ratify and affirm the Trust.

Date:

_____

Grantor

_____

Trustee

STATE OF _____

COUNTY OF _____

This instrument was acknowledged before me on this __ day of _____, 20__ by Grantor, _____ and Trustee, _____.

_____

Notary Public

My Commission Expires on:

Amendment to Trust

1, _____, ("Grantor") of _____, hereby amend _____ ("Trust") as follows: _____.

Except as expressly modified by this Amendment I approve, ratify and affirm the Trust.

Date:

_____
Grantor

_____
Trustee

STATE OF _____
COUNTY OF _____

This instrument was acknowledged before me on this __ day of _____, 20__ by Grantor, _____ and Trustee, _____.

_____
Notary Public

My Commission Expires on:

Amendment to Trust

1, _____, ("Grantor") of _____, hereby amend _____

("Trust") as follows: _____.

Except as expressly modified by this Amendment I approve, ratify and affirm the Trust.

Date:

_____

Grantor

_____

Trustee

STATE OF _____

COUNTY OF _____

This instrument was acknowledged before me on this __ day of _____, 20__ by Grantor,

_____ and Trustee, _____.

_____

Notary Public

My Commission Expires on:

Amendment to Trust

1, _____, ("Grantor") of _____, hereby amend _____ ("Trust") as follows: _____.

Except as expressly modified by this Amendment I approve, ratify and affirm the Trust.

Date:

_____

Grantor

_____

Trustee

STATE OF _____

COUNTY OF _____

This instrument was acknowledged before me on this __ day of _____, 20__ by Grantor, _____ and Trustee, _____.

_____

Notary Public

My Commission Expires on:

Amendment to Trust

1, _____, ("Grantor") of _____, hereby amend _____

("Trust") as follows: _____.

Except as expressly modified by this Amendment I approve, ratify and affirm the Trust.

Date:

_____

Grantor

_____

Trustee

STATE OF _____

COUNTY OF _____

This instrument was acknowledged before me on this __ day of _____, 20__ by Grantor,

_____ and Trustee, _____.

_____

Notary Public

My Commission Expires on:

Amendment to Trust

1, _____, ("Grantor") of _____, hereby amend _____

("Trust") as follows: _____.

Except as expressly modified by this Amendment I approve, ratify and affirm the Trust.

Date:

_____

Grantor

_____

Trustee

STATE OF _____

COUNTY OF _____

This instrument was acknowledged before me on this __ day of _____, 20__ by Grantor,

_____ and Trustee, _____.

_____

Notary Public

My Commission Expires on:

Amendment to Trust

1, _____, ("Grantor") of _____, hereby amend _____ ("Trust") as follows: _____.

Except as expressly modified by this Amendment I approve, ratify and affirm the Trust.

Date:

_____
Grantor

_____
Trustee

STATE OF _____
COUNTY OF _____

This instrument was acknowledged before me on this __ day of _____, 20__ by Grantor, _____ and Trustee, _____.

_____
Notary Public

My Commission Expires on:

Amendment to Trust

1, _____, ("Grantor") of _____, hereby amend _____

("Trust") as follows: _____.

Except as expressly modified by this Amendment I approve, ratify and affirm the Trust.

Date:

_____

Grantor

_____

Trustee

STATE OF _____

COUNTY OF _____

This instrument was acknowledged before me on this __ day of _____, 20__ by Grantor, _____ and Trustee, _____.

_____

Notary Public

My Commission Expires on:

Amendment to Trust

1, _____, ("Grantor") of _____, hereby amend _____

("Trust") as follows: _____.

Except as expressly modified by this Amendment I approve, ratify and affirm the Trust.

Date:

_____

Grantor

_____

Trustee

STATE OF _____

COUNTY OF _____

This instrument was acknowledged before me on this __ day of _____, 20__ by Grantor, _____ and Trustee, _____.

_____

Notary Public

My Commission Expires on:

Amendment to Trust

1, _____, ("Grantor") of _____, hereby amend _____

("Trust") as follows: _____.

Except as expressly modified by this Amendment I approve, ratify and affirm the Trust.

Date:

_____

Grantor

_____

Trustee

STATE OF _____

COUNTY OF _____

This instrument was acknowledged before me on this __ day of _____, 20__ by Grantor, _____ and Trustee, _____.

_____

Notary Public

My Commission Expires on:

Amendment to Trust

1, _____, ("Grantor") of _____, hereby amend _____ ("Trust") as follows: _____.

Except as expressly modified by this Amendment I approve, ratify and affirm the Trust.

Date:

_____

Grantor

_____

Trustee

STATE OF _____

COUNTY OF _____

This instrument was acknowledged before me on this __ day of _____, 20__ by Grantor, _____ and Trustee, _____.

_____

Notary Public

My Commission Expires on:

Amendment to Trust

1, _____, ("Grantor") of _____, hereby amend _____

("Trust") as follows: _____.

Except as expressly modified by this Amendment I approve, ratify and affirm the Trust.

Date:

_____

Grantor

_____

Trustee

STATE OF _____

COUNTY OF _____

This instrument was acknowledged before me on this __ day of _____, 20__ by Grantor, _____ and Trustee, _____.

_____

Notary Public

My Commission Expires on:

Amendment to Trust

1, _____, ("Grantor") of _____, hereby amend _____

("Trust") as follows: _____.

Except as expressly modified by this Amendment I approve, ratify and affirm the Trust.

Date:

_____

Grantor

_____

Trustee

STATE OF _____

COUNTY OF _____

This instrument was acknowledged before me on this __ day of _____, 20__ by Grantor,

_____ and Trustee, _____.

_____

Notary Public

My Commission Expires on:

Amendment to Trust

1, _____, ("Grantor") of _____, hereby amend _____

("Trust") as follows: _____.

Except as expressly modified by this Amendment I approve, ratify and affirm the Trust.

Date:

_____

Grantor

_____

Trustee

STATE OF _____

COUNTY OF _____

This instrument was acknowledged before me on this __ day of _____, 20__ by Grantor,

_____ and Trustee, _____.

_____

Notary Public

My Commission Expires on:

Amendment to Trust

1, _____, ("Grantor") of _____, hereby amend _____

("Trust") as follows: _____.

Except as expressly modified by this Amendment I approve, ratify and affirm the Trust.

Date:

_____

Grantor

_____

Trustee

STATE OF _____

COUNTY OF _____

This instrument was acknowledged before me on this __ day of _____, 20__ by Grantor, _____ and Trustee, _____.

_____

Notary Public

My Commission Expires on:

Amendment to Trust

1, _____, ("Grantor") of _____, hereby amend _____

("Trust") as follows: _____.

Except as expressly modified by this Amendment I approve, ratify and affirm the Trust.

Date:

_____

Grantor

_____

Trustee

STATE OF _____

COUNTY OF _____

This instrument was acknowledged before me on this __ day of _____, 20__ by Grantor,

_____ and Trustee, _____.

_____

Notary Public

My Commission Expires on:

Amendment to Trust

1, _____, ("Grantor") of _____, hereby amend _____

("Trust") as follows: _____.

Except as expressly modified by this Amendment I approve, ratify and affirm the Trust.

Date:

_____

Grantor

_____

Trustee

STATE OF _____

COUNTY OF _____

This instrument was acknowledged before me on this __ day of _____, 20__ by Grantor, _____ and Trustee, _____.

_____

Notary Public

My Commission Expires on:

Amendment to Trust

1, _____, ("Grantor") of _____, hereby amend _____ ("Trust") as follows: _____.

Except as expressly modified by this Amendment I approve, ratify and affirm the Trust.

Date:

_____
Grantor

_____
Trustee

STATE OF _____

COUNTY OF _____

This instrument was acknowledged before me on this __ day of _____, 20__ by Grantor, _____ and Trustee, _____.

_____
Notary Public

My Commission Expires on:

Amendment to Trust

1, _____, ("Grantor") of _____, hereby amend _____

("Trust") as follows: _____.

Except as expressly modified by this Amendment I approve, ratify and affirm the Trust.

Date:

_____

Grantor

_____

Trustee

STATE OF _____

COUNTY OF _____

This instrument was acknowledged before me on this __ day of _____, 20__ by Grantor, _____ and Trustee, _____.

_____

Notary Public

My Commission Expires on:

Amendment to Trust

1, _____, ("Grantor") of _____, hereby amend _____

("Trust") as follows: _____.

Except as expressly modified by this Amendment I approve, ratify and affirm the Trust.

Date:

_____

Grantor

_____

Trustee

STATE OF _____

COUNTY OF _____

This instrument was acknowledged before me on this __ day of _____, 20__ by Grantor, _____ and Trustee, _____.

_____

Notary Public

My Commission Expires on:

Amendment to Trust

1, _____, ("Grantor") of _____, hereby amend _____

("Trust") as follows: _____.

Except as expressly modified by this Amendment I approve, ratify and affirm the Trust.

Date:

_____

Grantor

_____

Trustee

STATE OF _____

COUNTY OF _____

This instrument was acknowledged before me on this __ day of _____, 20__ by Grantor,

_____ and Trustee, _____.

_____

Notary Public

My Commission Expires on:

Amendment to Trust

1, _____, ("Grantor") of _____, hereby amend _____

("Trust") as follows: _____.

Except as expressly modified by this Amendment I approve, ratify and affirm the Trust.

Date:

_____

Grantor

_____

Trustee

STATE OF _____

COUNTY OF _____

This instrument was acknowledged before me on this __ day of _____, 20__ by Grantor, _____ and Trustee, _____.

_____

Notary Public

My Commission Expires on:

Amendment to Trust

1, _____, ("Grantor") of _____, hereby amend _____ ("Trust") as follows: _____.

Except as expressly modified by this Amendment I approve, ratify and affirm the Trust.

Date:

_____

Grantor

_____

Trustee

STATE OF _____

COUNTY OF _____

This instrument was acknowledged before me on this __ day of _____, 20__ by Grantor, _____ and Trustee, _____.

_____

Notary Public

My Commission Expires on:

Amendment to Trust

1, _____, ("Grantor") of _____, hereby amend _____

("Trust") as follows: _____.

Except as expressly modified by this Amendment I approve, ratify and affirm the Trust.

Date:

_____

Grantor

_____

Trustee

STATE OF _____

COUNTY OF _____

This instrument was acknowledged before me on this __ day of _____, 20__ by Grantor, _____ and Trustee, _____.

_____

Notary Public

My Commission Expires on:

Amendment to Trust

1, _____, ("Grantor") of _____, hereby amend _____

("Trust") as follows: _____.

Except as expressly modified by this Amendment I approve, ratify and affirm the Trust.

Date:

_____

Grantor

_____

Trustee

STATE OF _____

COUNTY OF _____

This instrument was acknowledged before me on this __ day of _____, 20__ by Grantor, _____ and Trustee, _____.

_____

Notary Public

My Commission Expires on:

Amendment to Trust

1, _____, ("Grantor") of _____, hereby amend _____ ("Trust") as follows: _____.

Except as expressly modified by this Amendment I approve, ratify and affirm the Trust.

Date:

_____

Grantor

_____

Trustee

STATE OF _____

COUNTY OF _____

This instrument was acknowledged before me on this __ day of _____, 20__ by Grantor, _____ and Trustee, _____.

_____

Notary Public

My Commission Expires on:

Amendment to Trust

1, _____, ("Grantor") of _____, hereby amend _____

("Trust") as follows: _____.

Except as expressly modified by this Amendment I approve, ratify and affirm the Trust.

Date:

_____

Grantor

_____

Trustee

STATE OF _____

COUNTY OF _____

This instrument was acknowledged before me on this __ day of _____, 20__ by Grantor, _____ and Trustee, _____.

_____

Notary Public

My Commission Expires on:

Amendment to Trust

1, _____, ("Grantor") of _____, hereby amend _____

("Trust") as follows: _____.

Except as expressly modified by this Amendment I approve, ratify and affirm the Trust.

Date:

_____

Grantor

_____

Trustee

STATE OF _____

COUNTY OF _____

This instrument was acknowledged before me on this __ day of _____, 20__ by Grantor,

_____ and Trustee, _____.

_____

Notary Public

My Commission Expires on:

Amendment to Trust

1, _____, ("Grantor") of _____, hereby amend _____

("Trust") as follows: _____.

Except as expressly modified by this Amendment I approve, ratify and affirm the Trust.

Date:

_____

Grantor

_____

Trustee

STATE OF _____

COUNTY OF _____

This instrument was acknowledged before me on this __ day of _____, 20__ by Grantor, _____ and Trustee, _____.

_____

Notary Public

My Commission Expires on:

Amendment to Trust

1, _____, ("Grantor") of _____, hereby amend _____

("Trust") as follows: _____.

Except as expressly modified by this Amendment I approve, ratify and affirm the Trust.

Date:

_____

Grantor

_____

Trustee

STATE OF _____

COUNTY OF _____

This instrument was acknowledged before me on this __ day of _____, 20__ by Grantor, _____ and Trustee, _____.

_____

Notary Public

My Commission Expires on:

Amendment to Trust

1, _____, ("Grantor") of _____, hereby amend _____

("Trust") as follows: _____.

Except as expressly modified by this Amendment I approve, ratify and affirm the Trust.

Date:

_____

Grantor

_____

Trustee

STATE OF _____

COUNTY OF _____

This instrument was acknowledged before me on this __ day of _____, 20__ by Grantor,

_____ and Trustee, _____.

_____

Notary Public

My Commission Expires on:

Amendment to Trust

1, _____, ("Grantor") of _____, hereby amend _____ ("Trust") as follows: _____.

Except as expressly modified by this Amendment I approve, ratify and affirm the Trust.

Date:

_____

Grantor

_____

Trustee

STATE OF _____

COUNTY OF _____

This instrument was acknowledged before me on this __ day of _____, 20__ by Grantor, _____ and Trustee, _____.

_____

Notary Public

My Commission Expires on:

Amendment to Trust

1, _____, ("Grantor") of _____, hereby amend _____

("Trust") as follows: _____.

Except as expressly modified by this Amendment I approve, ratify and affirm the Trust.

Date:

_____

Grantor

_____

Trustee

STATE OF _____

COUNTY OF _____

This instrument was acknowledged before me on this __ day of _____, 20__ by Grantor,

_____ and Trustee, _____.

_____

Notary Public

My Commission Expires on:

Amendment to Trust

1, _____, ("Grantor") of _____, hereby amend _____ ("Trust") as follows: _____.

Except as expressly modified by this Amendment I approve, ratify and affirm the Trust.

Date:

_____

Grantor

_____

Trustee

STATE OF _____

COUNTY OF _____

This instrument was acknowledged before me on this __ day of _____, 20__ by Grantor, _____ and Trustee, _____.

_____

Notary Public

My Commission Expires on:

Amendment to Trust

1, _____, ("Grantor") of _____, hereby amend _____

("Trust") as follows: _____.

Except as expressly modified by this Amendment I approve, ratify and affirm the Trust.

Date:

_____

Grantor

_____

Trustee

STATE OF _____

COUNTY OF _____

This instrument was acknowledged before me on this __ day of _____, 20__ by Grantor, _____ and Trustee, _____.

_____

Notary Public

My Commission Expires on:

Amendment to Trust

1, _____, ("Grantor") of _____, hereby amend _____ ("Trust") as follows: _____.

Except as expressly modified by this Amendment I approve, ratify and affirm the Trust.

Date:

_____

Grantor

_____

Trustee

STATE OF _____

COUNTY OF _____

This instrument was acknowledged before me on this __ day of _____, 20__ by Grantor, _____ and Trustee, _____.

_____

Notary Public

My Commission Expires on:

Amendment to Trust

1, _____, ("Grantor") of _____, hereby amend _____ ("Trust") as follows: _____.

Except as expressly modified by this Amendment I approve, ratify and affirm the Trust.

Date:

_____
Grantor

_____
Trustee

STATE OF _____

COUNTY OF _____

This instrument was acknowledged before me on this __ day of _____, 20__ by Grantor, _____ and Trustee, _____.

_____
Notary Public

My Commission Expires on:

Made in the USA
Las Vegas, NV
27 March 2022